HORNCHURCH'S AIR HEROES
OF
THE FIRST WORLD WAR

HORNCHURCH'S AIR HEROES
OF
THE FIRST WORLD WAR

A PICTORIAL HISTORY
OF THE ROYAL FLYING CORPS
AT SUTTON'S FARM AIRFIELD 1915- 1919

Richard C. Smith

Mitor Publications

Published & typeset by
Mitor Publications
20 Theydon Gardens,
Rainham,
Essex
RM13 7TU
www.mitorpublications.co.uk

ISBN 978-0-9557180-4-5

Cover design by Ian Taylor
ian.taylor21@sky.com

Printed by Martins the Printers Limited
Sea View Works,
Spittal,
Berwick upon Tweed
TD15 1RS
www.martins-the-printers.co.uk

CONTENTS

ACKNOWLEDGEMENTS

I would like to thank the following people who helped in many ways to make the publication of this book possible, by supplying photographs and information within.

Sincere thanks goes to Air Marshal Sir Frederick Sowrey KCB, CBE, AFC; to First World War aviation historians John Barfoot and Ray Rimell. Thanks also to Tony Hibberd, No. 78 Squadron historian.
To the late Charles Shelley, for his memories of the airfield as a boy. To Barry Anderson in Switzerland, for the use of the propeller. To my good friend and acclaimed aviation artist Barry Weekley, for the use of his superb painting on the front cover depicting the destruction of Zeppelin L.32. The National Archive, Kew in London and the Imperial War Museum Photographic Archive in Lambeth. The RAF Museum, Hendon and the London Borough of Havering Library's Collection.

To Ian Taylor, my cover and photographic designer who pulled out all the stops on this one to provide an amazing cover and photographs once again. To Martins the Printers, for producing another superb book, many thanks.

To my wife Kim and my sons David and Robert, for their continuous support and love and finally to all my friends including John Ashford, Colin Lee, John Jones and Jonathon Steer and the general public who continue to support my work.

INTRODUCTION

It is nearly one hundred years as we approach the anniversary of the First World War, which saw nearly every nation on this planet thrown into a conflict which would have a profound impact on future generations in the twentieth century.

It was a war which for the first time saw the slaughter of armies by mechanised weapons on land, on the sea and in the air on a vast scale. With the first introduction of aeroplanes and airships used in the theatre of war, this led to the first bombing raids against military and civilian targets in history.

The first flight of an engine propelled aircraft had only taken place in 1903, when the American Wright Brothers recorded the first powered flight at Kittyhawk, North Carolina. Many other pioneering aviation engineers also produced basic aircraft and in 1909, the Frenchman, Louis Bleriot flew across the English Channel in his successful record breaking attempt on 25th July.

By the outbreak of war in August 1914, many countries had already established their own military air corps. In Britain, by 1912 there was the Royal Flying Corps. In Germany, the military had formed its own air force, Die Fliegertruppen des Deustschen Kaiserreiches the 'Imperial German Flying Corps' as well as using Zeppelin airships under the control of the German Naval Air Service, a small number of airships were also used by the German Army.

With the German advance through Belgium and into France and the beginning of stalemate on the western front, both sides began to dig in and trench warfare began; the use of aircraft first started by both sides sending over their pilots on reconnaissance patrols. The airmen defended themselves with revolvers and rifles if needed. As the conflict and technology progressed, the aircraft were fitted with machine guns and deadly duels between the pilots could be witnessed by the soldiers in the trenches below.

In January 1915, the use of giant airships against the British Isles was ordered by Kaiser Wilhelm, but attacks were to be against military targets only. Unfortunately, this was not adhered to and towns in Norfolk became the first to suffer civilian casualties by aerial bombing. The significance and effect of this bombing on the civilian population of Britain cannot be under estimated. Although the first raids had only killed a few people and wounded less than twenty; the fear that the German airships had inflicted, left many civilians in fear of their lives, as they waited every night expecting to hear the sound of the throbbing Zeppelin engines and bombs raining down on their own villages or towns.

The War Department took instant action in response to this new threat from the air and set up a defence of search-light and anti-aircraft gun batteries around various points that the airships were known to make landfall and provided protection for the larger towns and cities such as London.

The Royal Flying Corps would provide Home Defence Squadrons in the hope that they too would be able to shoot down the intruders over British skies. New airfields would have to be found and the search began in the south-east of England around Essex and Kent for suitable landing grounds.

This book tells the story of the airfield of Sutton's Farm in Hornchurch, Essex and how it provided the defence against the German Zeppelin and Gotha bomber raids between 1915 until 1918. This is a pictorial history and throughout this book the history is highlighted by photographs taken by professional and amateur photographers and some by the men and women who served there during this period. All are equally important images of history; every photograph has a story to tell. It is often said that 'a picture or photograph can say a thousand words,' and certainly the photographs in this book capture the essence and spirit of those early airmen and women, who devoted their lives in securing victory.

I hope this book will leave the reader, justly proud of their heritage and of that generation who sacrificed so much in order to keep this country and the world a free place to live.

'In the morning, we will remember them.'

Richard C. Smith July 2014

CHAPTER 1
'Threat from the Skies'

With the First World War only six months into the conflict, Britain was certainly unprepared for what would become the first aerial attack used against another nation in the history of warfare. In Germany, a new menacing weapon of war had been developed in the peacetime years; its creator Count Ferdinand von Zeppelin had envisaged the use of an airship for peaceful means of transport, but as the arms race increased during the early twentieth century and both Britain and Germany spent vast amounts on their armies and navies, the use of Zeppelin's airships were considered as possible weapons to inflict damage from the air.

Zeppelin was born on 8th July 1838 in Konstanz, a Grand Duchy of Baden., and attended a polytechnic school at Stuttgart until 1855, when he became a student at the military school at Ludwigsburg, appointed to the rank of lieutenant in 1858. He took time out from his military career to study science, engineering and chemistry at Tubingen.

In 1865, Zeppelin, then a young Prussian army officer, was sent to North America to be an official observer during the conflict between the Union and Confederate States during the American Civil War. Here he had witnessed the use of balloons as observation platforms which were used to see the opposing enemy positions of battle. On his return to Germany, his fascination with aerial machines and balloons became a full time occupation and he became fully involved with the development of building steerable airships that were powered by engines. On 2nd July 1900, Zeppelin had tested and made the first flight with LZ.1 over Lake Constance near Friedrichshafen in southern Germany. This was the beginning of Germany's airship development during the early twentieth century.

By 1914, the German airships had the capacity to travel large distances over land and sea and deliver bombs against the enemy. At the beginning of January 1915, the German Naval Command who operated the Zeppelins were given authority to begin operations to fly across the North Sea from their bases to bomb Britain; but it was firmly stipulated in the orders that only military targets were to be attacked. This would not remain the case.

The new German menace first arrived over Britain on the night of 19th/20th January 1915, when two airships, LZ.3 and LZ.4 dropped bombs on Sheringham, Snettisham, King's Lyn and Yarmouth in Norfolk. There were casualties on the ground, four killed and 16 injured, but the effect it had on the British population was to be far more significant. No longer were the British safe from the enemy across the Channel, protected by the 20 miles of water, which had previously seen the likes of the Spanish Armada and Napoleon Bonaparte stopped in their tracks, centuries before.

An instant reaction to the first raids, the War Office immediately set about in organising anti-aircraft batteries with search-light units around key points of the country, especially around the

London area. It also began a hurried search for suitable defensive airfield sites, which they hoped could be used to repel further attacks from raiding airships.

To this end, inspection groups were sent out to find the best areas of land which could be requisitioned by the Royal Flying Corps to use for home defensive squadrons to operate from. Several sites around the outskirts of London were selected; these included North Weald Basset near Epping, Hainault Farm, near Barkingside, Ilford, Joyce Green in Kent and at Hornchurch, Sutton's Farm.

The land at Sutton's Farm was owned by New College Oxford, who had held it for over six centuries. In 1915, it was being used for farming by tenant farmer Tom Crawford, and it consisted of 90 acres of fields that were flat and well drained and was being used for corn crops at the time. The land was deemed suitable by the inspection party and Royal Flying Corps officers that had been sent to investigate the area as a possible landing ground. It was officially requisitioned by the War Office and given over to the Royal Flying Corps. The scene was set for the arrival of a basic operational unit to be set up at Sutton's Farm.

On 3rd October 1915, local residents witnessed the arrival from Gosport of Captain A.G. Moore along with twelve men from No. 23 Squadron in one lorry, a light tender and provisions including bell tents for basic accommodation and aviation fuel.

The aircraft arrived later that day and consisted of two British Experimental 2c biplanes, supplied by the 5th Wing RFC at Gosport. Their pilots were Lieutenant E. Powell and Second Lieutenant H. O'Malley, both of No. 13 Squadron. The ground crew had the job of erecting the two RE5 canvas hangars for the aircraft, supplying fuel and armament, two bomb racks and eight 20lb bombs and anything else required to maintain a small operational unit.

The ground personnel were billeted in one of the local farmhouses, while the pilots were more comfortably housed in the local Hornchurch village public house, the White Hart, where their only means of communication to their commanders was by a newly installed telephone system, which was also relayed to the airfield.

By 8th October, two more pilots had arrived, Lieutenant R. Yates of 23 Squadron and from No. 14 Squadron, Lieutenant Jenkins. They relieved Powell and O'Malley.

The first action that the airfield undertook against the enemy came on the night of 13th October, when the Germans launched their largest raid of the war to date. Five Zeppelins had left their moorings at Nordholz in northern Germany and headed across the North Sea, four of them making landfall over the Norfolk, Suffolk coasts, while Zeppelin L.15 was sighted at 8.00 pm over Halstead, Essex, turning south-west for London. After dropping her bomb-load and causing the deaths of 72 civilians and many more injured, the airship headed back for Germany.

With the local air defences alerted, Sutton's Farm received a telephone communication to bring them at once into action. Early that day, a young 18-year old pilot has just arrived at Sutton's to take up his posting; his name was Lieutenant John Slessor.

At 9.05 pm Slessor was ordered aloft immediately in his biplane to begin his patrol and begin his 40-minute climb to an altitude of 10,000 feet in order to start his search for the raider. The aircraft of this period were extremely basic with only a few instruments on the dashboard, no heating or oxygen facilities and no radio or navigation communication.

When Slessor finally saw the giant airship it had been caught in the beams of the local searchlight batteries. But as he was about to make his approach towards it, it disappeared into a cloud bank and after much searching, he decided he had lost it. His patrol had taken him two hours and he was now running low on fuel. He returned to Sutton's Farm, which had been lit up by the ground personnel using old petrol cans filled with cotton waste material and soaked in petrol as a primitive flare path.

Unfortunately, Slessor damaged his aircraft's undercarriage due to a heavy landing and being blinded for a few seconds by a searchlight crew, who although well intentioned with the idea of illuminating his aircraft, actually hindered his approach. This had been Slessor's first operational flight; he was also recorded as the first British pilot to intercept an enemy airship over the United Kingdom.

The airship raids continued into 1916, with still no real success by the Home Defence Squadrons in bringing down the raiders. One of the many problems was having the right equipment to get the job done, especially the armament, which consisted of a Lewis machine gun, which in effect would spray the Zeppelin with 0.303 bullets. These would pass through the fabric of the airship, but could be easily repaired by the some of the Zeppelin crew who were sail-makers and repaired any damage by using quick sealing patches over the ruptured fabric.

Help was on hand however when an Australian named John Pomeroy invented the explosive bullet as did Squadron Commander F.A. Brock. The new ammunition which could blow large holes into the fabric and then ignite the hydrogen gases seemed the ideal solution to bring down the giant intruders. By early 1916, the War Office proceeded to order the supply of one million rounds of the new ammunition for all .303 calibre machine guns to be used by the Home Defence squadrons.

Further Zeppelin sightings by pilots stationed at Sutton's Farm continued. On the night of 31st March 1916, Second Lieutenant E. W Powell while on patrol sighted Zeppelin L.15, the same machine that had evaded John Slessor a few months earlier, and this could be seen at the height of 8,500 feet. It was commanded by Lieutenant Commander Joachim Breithaupt, who was now turning south-south-west on to the Thames, passing over Orsett, Essex. The time of Powell's sighting was around 9 pm, but he was unable to intercept, because he was too far away. The airship was not destined to escape however; Lieutenant Claude Ridley operating from the airfield at Joyce Green was able to close in enough to fire off a burst from his machine gun before losing it in the darkness as the searchlights swung away.

L15 was caught again in searchlights as it drifted over the Thames between Erith and Purfleet and was eventually hit by the gun battery at Purfleet which opened a large gash. L15 continued its journey and at 9.40 pm dropped 20 high explosive and 24 incendiary bombs into the open fields at Wennington and Rainham in order to lighten the load and gain extra height.

The Zeppelin was finally brought down by Second Lieutenant Alfred de Bathe Brandon from Hainault Farm airfield causing serious damage to the L15. Trying to make its way towards the Channel the airship finally ditched offshore near the Kent Knock Lighthouse, near Margate. Most of her crew were rescued by the armed trawler 'Olivine' before she sank, after efforts to bring her ashore failed.

On 15th April 1916, it was decided that the various squadrons that were situated around London should be formed into the 39th Home Defence Squadron under the command of Major T.C. R.

Higgins, who moved his headquarters from Hounslow to Woodford Green.

At Sutton's Farm, the airfield was rapidly improving its facilities with new timber hangars and brick buildings being constructed, making operational life a lot more bearable. The arrival of new pilots and aircraft also helped to increase the morale, and by then the airfield had six serviceable aircraft.

Among the new arrivals were Lieutenant William Leefe Robinson, who became flight commander of B Flight; two young pilots, Lieutenants Frederick Sowrey and Wulstan Tempest joined him in early June. They immediately struck up a friendship and were to become the most successful team of airmen stationed at Sutton's.

The brilliant German airship designer Count Ferdinand von Zeppelin, whose creation was turned into a weapon of war by the German High Command when the First World War began in August 1914.

The mighty German Zeppelin airship. At 650 feet in length it was an awesome sight to behold viewed from the ground as well as from the air. This photograph shows the L. 32. Author's collection

A view showing the village high street of Hornchurch, circa 1916/17. Author's collection

The damage inflicted on one of the houses at Great Yarmouth by the first Zeppelin raid on Britain over the night of 19th/20th January 1915.

Author's collection

This wartime poster was issued to raise awareness to the public and identify the various aircraft and airships being flown by both sides in the conflict.

Author's collection

A view of the wooden hangar sheds at Sutton's Farm in 1916, which housed the BE2c aircraft of No. 39 Squadron.

F. Sowrey collection

Three pilot friends of 39 (Home Defence) Squadron pictured walking arm in arm at the airfield. Left to right: Lieutenants Wulstan Tempest, Leefe Robinson and Frederick Sowrey.(Note the wooden farm buildings and hangar behind)

F. Sowrey collection

CHAPTER 2
'First Victory'

On the night of 25th April, another Zeppelin alert was called and Leefe Robinson was ordered to take off. He climbed to an altitude of 8,000 feet and sighted the Zeppelin LZ.97 some 2,000 feet above his position. He opened fire without success as his tracer bullets fell short of his target and the airship began to out climb him to safety. Robinson returned to the airfield somewhat disappointed with the outcome. His luck was to change however five months later, when on the night of 2nd/3rd September 1916, he would make history.

On this night, the German Army airship SL.11 left its base to fly across the North Sea to make landfall at Foulness at 11.40 pm. The airship was not designated a Zeppelin, but a Schutte-Lanz, being made of a wooden frame construction, unlike the Zeppelins which were made of metal. Its commander Captain Wilhelm Schramm steered his machine on a new course to avoid the Thames defences, which were now well known.

Schramm approached London from a northerly direction, travelling over Hertfordshire and was seen over St. Albans at 1.10 am, finally dropping his bombs on London Colney, then at Enfield and Edmonton before being caught in the searchlight beams over Wood Green. The SL.11 was then engaged by the ground defences, which opened fire, but achieved no success.

Earlier that evening at around 11.00 pm, the telephone had rung at Leefe Robinson's bedside and he was ordered to 'Take air-raid action.' His aircraft, a BE2c was wheeled out of its hangar on to the field and made ready for take-off. Because Sutton's Farm was near to the Thames, it was always dogged by fog and mist in late autumn and winter. That night was no exception, so mechanics and ground staff were busy lighting Money flares, which consisted of asbestos and paraffin, and burned longer than the old method of buckets filled with petrol.

Robinson dressed in his leather flying helmet and leather jacket climbed into his cockpit and checked his Lewis machine gun mounted above the top wing; the mechanic swung the propeller and the engine coughed into life. Robinson checked his instrument dials, while the ground crew removed the chocks from the wheels. He opened up the throttle and his aircraft accelerated down the field and rose into the air.

Meanwhile, the SL.11 was making her way back home, crossing over the Thames, south-east of Woolwich at about 1.00 am.

The following is the official report given by Robinson on his engagement with the Zeppelin that night.

I have the honour to make the following report on the night patrol made by myself on the 2nd/3rd instant.

I went up at 11.08 on the night of the 2nd, with instructions to patrol between Sutton's and Joyce

Green. I climbed to 10,000 feet in 53 minutes. I counted what I thought to be ten sets of flares, there were clouds below me, but on the whole it was a beautiful clear night.

I saw nothing until about 1.10 am, when two searchlights picked out a Zeppelin southeast of Woolwich. The clouds had collected in this quarter and the searchlights had some difficulty in keeping up with the aircraft. By the time I had managed to climb to 12,900 feet and I made in the direction of the Zeppelin, which was being fired on by a few anti-aircraft guns, hoping to cut it off on its way eastward.

I slowly gained on it for about ten minutes, I judged it to be about 200 feet below me and I sacrificed my speed in order to keep my height. It went behind some clouds, avoided the searchlights and I lost sight of it. After about fifteen minutes of fruitless search, I returned to my patrol.

I managed to pick up and distinguish my flares again. At about 1.50 am, I noticed a red glow in the northeast of London. Taking it to be an outbreak of fire, I went in that direction. At 2.05 am, a Zeppelin was picked up by a searchlight over north, northeast of London.

Remembering my last failure, I sacrificed height (I was still at 12,000 feet) for speed and made a nose down for the Zeppelin. I saw shells bursting and night tracers' shells flying around it. When I drew closer, I noticed that the anti-aircraft fire was too high or too low, also a good many rose 800 feet behind – a few tracers went right over. I could hear the bursts when about 3,000 feet from the Zeppelin.

I flew about 800 feet below it from bow to stern and distributed one drum of ammunition along it, but it seemed to have no effect. I then got behind it (by then I was close to 500 feet or less below) and concentrated one drum on one part beneath. I was then at a height of 11,500 feet, when attacking the Zeppelin.

I had hardly finished the drum when I saw the part fired at begin to glow. In a few seconds the whole rear part was blazing. When the third drum was fired there were no searchlights on the Zeppelin and the anti-aircraft guns had stopped firing. I quickly got out of the way of the falling blazing Zeppelin, and being very excited fired off a few Very lights and dropped a parachute flare. Having very little oil or petrol left I returned to Sutton's Farm, landing at 2.45 am. On landing I found that I had shot away the machine gun wire guard, the rear part of the centre section and had pierced the rear main spar several times.

The blazing wreck of the SL11 could be seen falling from the night sky from Staines to Southend. All over London people who had witnessed the fall of the airship began cheering and crying out *God Save the King*' as the giant ball of flame continued its descent, finally crashing at Cuffley, just north of Enfield, behind the Plough public house in a beet field, where it burned on the ground for nearly two hours. Wilhelm Schramm and all his crew perished.

Once he had landed, Robinson who was totally exhausted and could hardly speak because of the cold, he was met by Lieutenant Sowrey and taken to a small office, which had been made out of old aircraft packing casing. He was given a large cup of cocoa by a clerk, after which he wrote down his report and then went straight back to his camp-bed in the hangar and immediately fell asleep. He was evidently somewhat annoyed, when at dawn he was awoken by Sowrey, who said he would take him to the site of the crashed Zeppelin. Robinson shouted *For God's sake, can't a chap get to sleep in on a Sunday morning?* Nevertheless he went to Cuffley and examined the remains of SL.11, and was swamped by people wishing him all the best, shaking hands and patting him on the back. He stated later: *'My back is black and blue from all the thumps the crowd gave me.'*

The railways laid on special trains from King's Cross to carry an estimated 10,000 people to see the wreck at Cuffley. The bodies of the crew were initially placed under a tarpaulin, before being taken away and given a military funeral with Royal Flying Corps officers carrying the coffin of Captain Schramm, to the village churchyard of Essendon. They would remain there until they were exhumed in July 1966, and re-interred at Cannock Chase, Staffordshire, where the German dead of both World Wars now lie in the German military cemetery.

William Leefe Robinson had now become a national hero and on 9th September he was awarded the Victoria Cross medal, which he was presented with by King George V at Windsor Castle.

His photograph appeared in all the newspapers and magazines of the day, and he was recognised by crowds of people wherever he went. Even in his favourite restaurant in London, the Piccadilly Grill, where he would go to hear his favourite singer, Violet Essex, he could not be left alone, drawing the attention of the audience from the singing star. Money too had also come his way. British businessmen had contributed large amounts of cash as rewards for the first airman to shoot down a Zeppelin over Britain; this amounted to £3,500.

At Sutton's Farm life would never be quite the same again, and the people of Hornchurch found new fame as they referred to 'our aerodrome.' There were frequent visits to the airfield by young single ladies who were invited to take tea or a tour of the airfield by the young officers, including Robinson, who now had been promoted to captain.

Many villagers would often catch a glimpse of Robinson and Sowrey driving in a new Prince Henry Vauxhall car, which Robinson had purchased with some of his prize money.

On Saturday 16th September, there was yet another airship alert. Again Robinson was the pilot on duty for that evening, but whilst taking off down the field, his aircraft crashed into the boundary hedge. He escaped unhurt from the aircraft, which proceeded to catch fire and was completely destroyed. This was the same aircraft he had brought down the SL.11.

James Anderson was licensee of the 'Plough' public house in Cranham, a few miles from Sutton's Farm. Anderson was also a master carpenter by trade and was invited to become a civilian employee at the airfield, where his work was repairing the wooden airframes, struts and propellers of the fighters stationed there. His grandson Barry recalls his grandfather's stories of his time there.

He told me how the pilots would visit the 'Plough' pub which had become a popular watering hole, especially at weekends for military men of all descriptions. Fortunately, the 'Plough' was conveniently situated just a mile outside the restricted war zone that included Sutton's Farm and Warley Barracks, where drinking was forbidden.

One of his most vivid memories was when two weeks after William Leefe Robinson had shot down the first German airship over British soil; he was on duty at the airfield and the weather had been atrocious for some days previously. That day, it fell to Robinson to undertake a patrol in the same aircraft he had shot down the German airship; unfortunately, he began sinking into heavy mud as he throttled the engine and while attempting to take-off in his aircraft the wheels became rutted in the muddy quagmire. The sheer power of the engine thrust the biplane not upwards, but forwards flipping the nose over and smashing the four-bladed propeller into the ground, coming to a sudden halt by the boundary fence. At that moment, the whole aircraft structure burst into flames. Robinson managed to jump out uninjured. Soon the brave little plane turned into a mass of burnt cinders and molten metal with the exception of some solid sections of the broken wooden propeller embedded in the mud, the rest of the aircraft was written off.

With considerable foresight, my grandfather retrieved the shattered broken and burnt propeller and eventually gave the relic to my father for safe keeping. It is now part of our family's heritage.

Robinson remained with 39 Squadron into early 1917, before being posted at his own request to serve in France as a flight commander with No. 48 Squadron in March 1917, flying the new Bristol F2 fighter. On 4th April, he led a flight of six aircraft on a reconnaissance patrol around the Douai area and when arriving over it, they were attacked by German aircraft of Jasta II, the renowned squadron led by the famous German ace Manfred Von Richthofen. During combat that ensued, Robinson and his observer Lieutenant Edward Warburton had their aircraft badly damaged from bullets fired by an Albatross biplane flown by Sergeant Sebastian Festner and they were forced to crash-land.

For several weeks, the fate of Robinson and Warburton was unknown to the authorities and they were listed as missing in action. It was not until 25th April, that news arrived that he and his colleague were still alive and in German hands. He was sent to the prisoner of war camp at Freiburg and it was from here in September 1917, together with several other officers, they escaped through a window of one of the prison wings; but were captured again almost immediately.

Robinson made another four escape attempts before being sent to the camp at Clausthal in the Harz Mountains, before finally going to Holzminden in July 1918. Here he received harsh treatment from the camp commandant Heinrich Neimayer, who singled him out for ceaseless and methodical persecution.

At war's end in November 1918, Robinson returned to Britain in very poor health following the months of harsh treatment inflicted upon him by his captors. In December 1918, with Britain and most of Europe hit by a massive Spanish Flu pandemic, he was already weakened and became a victim of the illness. He was staying at the home of friends, Nancy and Edward Clifton, when he passed away on 31st December 1918, aged 24.

He was given a full military funeral and hundreds of people turned out to pay their respects as his coffin was carried through the streets on a gun-carriage. He was buried at All Saints' Churchyard at Harrow Weald. A memorial was later erected to Robinson at the site where the airship crashed as a fitting tribute to a gallant airman. His Victoria Cross and medals can now be viewed in the Lord Ashcroft Gallery within the Imperial War Museum in London, while a public house in Harrow Weald is named the William Leefe Robinson and in Hornchurch a road named Robinson Close pays tribute to his courage and exploits whilst flying from Sutton's Farm.

Early aviation was extremely risqué and many accidents occurred as demonstrated in this photograph showing a BE2c biplane which has nosed in. The aircraft 4110 was used by 19 Flying Reserve Squadron at the airfield and was being flown by William Leefe Robinson on 4th February 1916, when the accident occurred.

RAF Museum collection

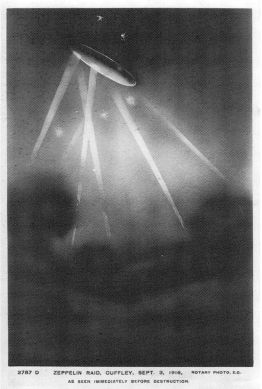

3787 D   ZEPPELIN RAID, CUFFLEY, SEPT. 3, 1916,   ROTARY PHOTO, E.C.
AS SEEN IMMEDIATELY BEFORE DESTRUCTION.

Two postcard's of the time depicting the shooting down of the Schutte Lanz airship SL11 by William Leefe Robinson over Cuffley on the night of the 2nd/3rd September 1916.
Author's collection

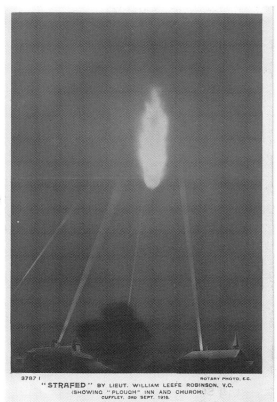

3787 I   ROTARY PHOTO, E.C.
"STRAFED" BY LIEUT. WILLIAM LEEFE ROBINSON, V.C.
(SHOWING "PLOUGH" INN AND CHURCH),
CUFFLEY, 3RD SEPT. 1916.

22

Commander of the Schutte- Lanz airship SL.11, Hauptmann Wilhelm Schramm, who perished along with his crew after the attack by William Leefe Robinson. He was actually born in England at Old Charlton, Kent on 11th December 1885. His father was a director of the Siemens Electrical Company and the London representative. With his father's death in 1900, Wilhelm returned to live in Germany, where he eventually took up a military career.   Albatros Publications/Ray Rimell

Lieutenant Robinson is pictured in the cockpit of his BE2c biplane, Serial No. 2693 the following day after shooting down the German airship. His ground crew stand with part of the aircraft's centre top wing section which was damaged during the action.   F. Sowrey collection

The ground personnel of Sutton's Farm cheer their new hero following his achievement over the 'Hun' that September night, the first victory over the German airships.   Author's collection

Robinson with his fellow pilots pictured in front of his aircraft. Left to right: Lieutenant Cecil Durstan, Frederick Sowrey, Robinson, Captain Stammers and Wulstan Tempest.   F. Sowrey collection

THE DAILY MIRROR, Monday, September 4, 1916.

13 ZEPPELINS ATTACK ENGLAND—THOUSANDS SEE A RAIDER'S DOOM

The Daily Mirror

CERTIFIED CIRCULATION LARGER THAN THAT OF ANY OTHER DAILY PICTURE PAPER

No. 4,014. | Registered at the G.P.O. as a Newspaper. | MONDAY, SEPTEMBER 4, 1916 | One Halfpenny.

BLAZING ZEPPELIN CRASHES TO EARTH NEAR ENFIELD: ONLY FIFTEEN CASUALTIES IN "THE MOST FORMIDABLE ATTACK."

Men of the Royal Flying Corps examining the wrecked engine. The spot where the car fell, follows strewn with money.

"Tommies" sorting out the wreckage.

The policemen lent a hand.

What is officially described as the most formidable Zeppelin attack yet made on this country took place on Saturday night and early yesterday morning. Thirteen airships took part, but only three were able to approach the outskirts of London, and of these one was destroyed. It was heavily engaged by anti-aircraft guns and aeroplanes, and after a few minutes was seen to burst into flame and fall rapidly towards the earth. And the casualties are only two killed and thirteen injured.—(*Daily Mirror* photographs.)

The front pages of the victory by Leefe Robinson was headline news for many days following. The Daily Mirror carried this front page showing photographs of the remains of the downed airship. Inside a double centre spread continued with coverage of the great event.

Author's collection

GREAT BRITISH BLOWS AT FOE ON THE SOMME AND IN EAST AFRICA

The Daily Mirror

CERTIFIED CIRCULATION LARGER THAN THAT OF ANY OTHER DAILY PICTURE PAPER

No. 4,015. | Registered at the G.P.O. as a Newspaper. | TUESDAY, SEPTEMBER 5, 1916 | One Halfpenny.

THE CUFFLEY PILGRIMS: WHAT THEY WENT THROUGH IN ORDER TO SEE THE FRAGMENTS OF THE GASBAG.

The return home. Many travelled standing on the buffers while thousands were stranded and besieged the telephones begging for taxicabs to be sent out to them.

Lady Diana Manners looking for relics.

A rough passage. Difficulties and rain did not keep them back. They meant to get there somehow.

London probably has never seen a stranger pilgrimage than that which poured along the roads leading northwards in the half-light of Sunday morning. Some thought Highgate was the goal, others, less optimistic, suggested Hendon, but none thought of Cuffley; in fact, ten per cent. of them had probably never heard of the place which has had greatness thrust upon it so suddenly. They all found it eventually, but as the numbers kept on swelling throughout the day the difficulty was to get home at night.

Hoards of inquisitive sightseer's make their way to Cuffley to view the remains of the German airship.

Author's collection

SPLENDID BRITISH GAINS IN GREAT NEW ADVANCE

The Daily Mirror

CERTIFIED CIRCULATION LARGER THAN THAT OF ANY OTHER DAILY PICTURE PAPER

No. 4,016. | Registered at the G.P.O. as a Newspaper. | WEDNESDAY, SEPTEMBER 6, 1916 | One Halfpenny.

LORD FRENCH EXAMINES GASBAG RELIC.

V.C. FOR MAN WHO SAVED WOMEN AND CHILDREN BY DESTROYING ZEPP.

The nose piece, which was cut away.

Lieutenant Robinson. He is only twenty-one, but has made a speciality of night flying.

Lord French climbs on the wheel to have a look.

Cheering the intrepid pilot as he drove away from the scene of the wreck on Sunday evening.

Field-Marshal Lord French visited the War Office yesterday to see an important part of one of the enemy airships which raided England on the 2nd-3rd inst. There is no doubt that it had suffered severe damage from gunfire. The relic in question was picked up in the Eastern Counties.—(*Daily Mirror* and L.N.A.)

Lieutenant William Leefe Robinson (Worcester Regiment and Royal Flying Corps) has been awarded the V.C. for most conspicuous bravery, described in last night's *Gazette* as follows:—"He attacked an enemy airship under circumstances of great difficulty and danger, and sent it crashing to the ground in a flaming wreck. He had been in the air for more than two hours, and had previously attacked another airship during his flight." This announcement thus solves the secret of the burning mass of Sunday morning.

The Daily Mirror for September 6th carried the news that William Leefe Robinson was to be awarded the Victoria Cross for his action and courage against SL.11   Author's Collection

27

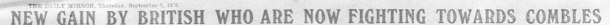

NEW GAIN BY BRITISH WHO ARE NOW FIGHTING TOWARDS COMBLES

The Daily Mirror

CERTIFIED CIRCULATION LARGER THAN THAT OF ANY OTHER DAILY PICTURE PAPER

| No. 4,017. | Registered at the G.P.O. as a Newspaper. | THURSDAY, SEPTEMBER 7, 1916 | One Halfpenny. |

THE ROYAL FLYING CORPS BURY THEIR FALLEN FOES: FUNERAL OF THE CREW OF THE ZEPPELIN L 21.

The service at the graveside. It was very brief, and concluded with the sounding of "The Last Post."

Royal Flying Corps officers carrying the commander's coffin.

Leaving Cuffley. The funeral procession was of a severely simple nature.

Crowd trying to gain admission to the cemetery, which was strongly guarded by police.

Passing through the village. There was nothing resembling military show.

The funeral of the sixteen incinerated Germans, who perished with their craft, took place at Potters Bar yesterday, the coffins being conveyed by motor-wagon along the four miles of country road which separates Cuffley from the cemetery. There were two graves—one 25ft. long and 7ft. wide, in which the crew were buried, while there was a separate one for the commander. A brass plate on his coffin gave the number of the raider as L 21.—(*Daily Mirror* photographs.)

The newspaper coverage continued with photographs showing the funeral service and burial of the German airship crew, who all perished that fateful night in September. Author's collection

Francis H. Maskell served at Sutton's Farm as Leefe Robinson's mechanic. He was initially transferred from the Somerset Light Infantry. Maskell can be seen in the crowd of airmen celebrating Robinson's victory on page 8.

W. Bernard collection

The car carrying William Leefe Robinson is pictured leaving Windsor Castle on 9th September 1916 following his meeting with King George V and his award of the Victoria Cross. Crowds lined the roads leading up to the castle and cheers and applause greeted him on the route.

Author's collection

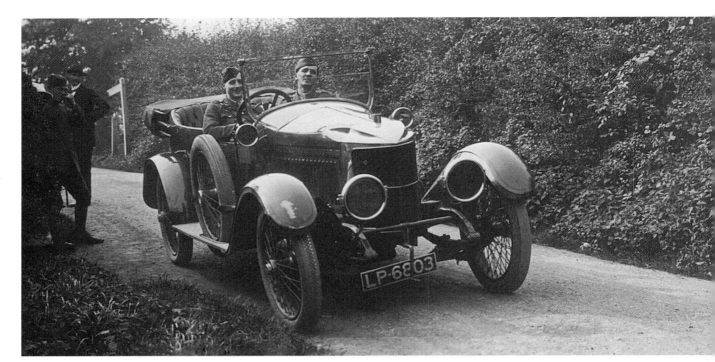

Robinson and Sowrey pictured travelling down Sutton's Lane, Hornchurch in the Prince Henry Vauxhall that Robinson bought from the 'prize' money he received from a number of generou patrons following the shooting down of the airship.

F. Sowrey collectio

The two pilots take time to chat with a well-wisher at Hornchurch.

F. Sowrey collectio

On the night of 16th September, Robinson was ordered to take-off on a night patrol. On getting airborne his aircraft crashed into a hedgerow and burst into flames; fortunately Robinson escaped unscathed, but his aircraft was destroyed. Here an airman is pictured with the remains of the tail-section.

F. Sowrey collection

The officers of No. 39 (Home Defence) Squadron line up for a group photograph: left to right standing are:
Captain Robert Stammers,
Second Lieutenant Wulstan Tempest DSO,
Lieutenants Leefe Robinson VC
Frederick Sowrey DSO,
Major H. A. Morton. Seated:
Lieutenants C.C. Brock,
Cecil Durstan and P. Russell Mallinson

F. Sowrey collection

CHAPTER 3
'Knights of the Air'

Just two weeks later, following the excitement of Leefe Robinson's shooting down of the first German airship, Sutton's Farm again would be headline news. On the night of 23rd/24th September 1916, it was the turn of Lieutenant Frederick Sowrey to write himself into the history books.

Two Zeppelins, L.32 commanded by Oberleutnant Werner Peterson and L.33 by Kapitanleutnant Alois Bocker, were among eleven German naval airships sent out from Germany that night to raid between the north of the Wash and as far as London.

Early that afternoon at around 4 pm Sowrey and Leefe Robinson were taking tea at the home of Major Morton and his wife at Woodford. Major Morton was called to the telephone and was asked to tell his two guests to return to Sutton's Farm immediately, as an alert had been received that there was to be a raid that evening. It was not until 9 pm that both pilots received orders to stand ready; Sowrey was to take the first patrol.

The two Zeppelins had crossed the North Sea and had moved inland; L.32 reached Tunbridge Wells by 12.10 am on 24th September. It then turned northwards dropping a sighting flare at 12.30 am. At 12.50 am, it was caught in a searchlight beam over Swanley Junction; although the Zeppelin dropped its bombs on the searchlight battery, it missed it. It continued over the town of Dartford and crossed the River Thames, east of Purfleet, where it came under fire from gun-positions situated between Beacon Hill and Tunnel Farm. The Zeppelin again answered by dropping nine high-explosive bombs and six incendiaries, which fell at Aveley.

At 11.25 pm Lieutenant Sowrey had received orders to take-off and patrol between the airfield and Joyce Green in Kent. By 1.00 am, the L.32 had dropped her entire bomb load and was now heading back home. Sowrey's first-hand account of what happened during the patrol, relates the following details:

The weather was fine and clear with a few thin clouds at around 3,000 feet. At a height of 4,000 feet, I passed another machine going in a northerly direction, I was then flying south. I continued climbing as hard as possible and at 12.10 am I noticed an enemy airship in a southerly direction. It appeared to be over Woolwich. I made for the airship at once, but before I reached it the searchlights had lost it.

I was at this time at 8,000 feet, there was a certain amount of gunfire, but it was not intense. I continued to climb and reached an altitude of 13,000 feet. At 12.45 am I noticed an airship in an easterly direction and at once made in this direction and manoeuvred into position beneath it.

The airship was now well lit by searchlights, but there was no sign of gunfire I could distinctly see the propellers revolving as the airship manoeuvred to avoid the searchlight beams. I began firing at it. The first two drums of ammunition had apparently no effect, but the third caused the envelope to catch fire in several places, in the centre and front. All firing was traversing along the length of the airship. Ammunition was loaded with a mixture of Brock and Pomeroy tracer.

I watched the burning airship fall and strike the ground, and then proceeded to fire my red flares. I landed back at Sutton's Farm.

Sowrey's machine gun fire had in fact hit one of the cylinder petrol tanks stowed along the length of the Zeppelin's central walkway. In seconds it had engulfed the airship, sending it crashing down to fall to earth at Snail's Hall Farm, Great Burstead, near Billericay, Essex.

All the crew perished; Commander Werner Peterson's body was found some distance away from the wreckage. He had obviously jumped to his death, rather than being burnt alive.

After landing back at Sutton's Farm in his BE2c No.4112 at 1.40 am, Sowrey was met and congratulated by Robinson and Captain Frederick Bowers and given a hot drink. He then contacted Major Morton at Headquarters Woodford Green, passing on his information and asking to go to the crash-site and inspect the remains of the airship later that morning.

Both Sowrey and Robinson along with Captains Bowers and Stammers and Lieutenant Cyril Durstan, jumped into Robinson's Prince Henry Vauxhall and began the journey to Great Burstead.

The people of Hornchurch, who had witnessed the fall of the L.32, cheered as the pilots passed through the village. By the time Sowrey and his group had arrived at the crash-site, the area had been cordoned off by soldiers, to stop any members of the public from getting too near the wreckage. Heated words were in fact exchanged, when an army officer refused Sowrey entrance through, until he was told that this was the airman who had shot the airship down.

As with Robinson's airship, thousands of people made the trip to view the downed airship, travelling by road and rail; many picking up pieces of the Zeppelin's shattered metal framework as souvenirs. The public were even charged a fee of 2d to gain admission to the site; proceeds went to the Red Cross Funds and about £80 was collected. Other people who inspected the site included high-ranking officials including David Lloyd George, shortly to become Prime Minister and Arthur Balfour who was with the Admiralty.

For his heroic actions Frederick Sowrey was awarded the Distinguished Service Order.

One eye witness who was then just thirteen years old was Ronald Shelly of Billericay. Interviewed by the author in 1994, at the age of 91, he remembered:

I saw both the Zeppelins come down in flames, the one at Cuffley and Billericay. My father brought me over to see the remains of the L.32. It was a Saturday, I remember all the people and anyone who had a car at that time was blowing their horns and cheering. The country lanes were completely clogged up with people, coming and going from the site. Luckily, the airship had missed the village otherwise it would have been burnt to the ground.

Air Marshal Sir Frederick Sowrey, the son of Lieutenant Frederick Sowrey also recalls his father's memories of this time:

My father often spoke about the difficulties of night-flying during this particular time; they were in fact the very first night-fighters. There was no cockpit lighting for the instruments; he had a torch hanging around his neck on a lanyard with the battery tucked into his tunic pocket. He talked about the problems in finding the landing ground after a patrol, no aids as such, no radio, just visual, looking over the side of the aircraft trying to identify landmarks by moonlight, if it was a clear night, or looking for a flare path.

They operated at altitudes where these days you would use oxygen and the cold was very intense. For this, the pilots pay was the princely sum of ten shillings a day.

He was very appreciative of his ground-crew, and insisted that when photographs of himself were taken by his aircraft, the morning after the Zeppelin had been shot down that his crew were in the photograph as well. They looked a bit embarrassed about being in the limelight, but he wanted them to share in some of the glory he had achieved, to rub off on them as well.

Another Zeppelin, L.33 had also been destroyed that night, being shot down by a pilot flying from Hainault Farm, Lieutenant Alfred Brandon. This Zeppelin did not go down in flames as the previous ones had, but crash-landed at Little Wigborough, Essex. Not wishing it to fall into enemy hands, the crew set light to it, and then proceeded to walk through the country lanes in regimental order to find the local or military authorities to whom they could surrender themselves. They were finally apprehended by a local policeman and marched into captivity.

There would be one more final success against the Zeppelins from one of the pilots at Sutton's Farm. This took place on the night of 1st/2nd October 1916, when ten Zeppelins were sent to attack towns and cities in the Midlands, Norfolk, Lincolnshire and London. One of these airships L.31 was commanded by the renowned Zeppelin commander Heinrich Mathy. As the Zeppelin approached London, the alert sounded and the Home Defence Squadrons prepared to go into action once again. Lieutenant Wulstan Tempest was a good friend and colleague of Robinson and Sowrey; he had earlier that day flown over to North Weald to meet friends and decided to stay for dinner at Epping. He was also on patrol duty that evening and decided to begin this from North Weald. Now informed about the incoming threat, Tempest was ordered to begin his patrol at 11.00 pm.

By 11.45 pm, Tempest had climbed to an altitude of 14,000 feet and was over the south-west of London; below there was a heavy fog with the beams of searchlights penetrating up through the mist. He then turned his head north-east, where he could see the outline of Zeppelin L.31 against the illuminated sky. The ground defences had opened fire causing the Zeppelin to take evasive measures and start to climb, to avoid the barrage of exploding shells.

Tempest continued to pursue at about 15,000 feet. He was about five miles behind the airship when his aircraft's fuel pressure pump decided to break down, causing the flow of petrol to his engine to dry up. He had no option but to operate the hand pump to keep up the pressure in his petrol tank, while operating the rest of the aircraft's flying controls with his other hand. He was now becoming very exhausted as he finally came within range of the giant airship.

The gun batteries below had almost ceased firing as L.33 moved out of range. What happened next is drawn from Tempest's official report:

As I drew up to the Zeppelin, to my relief I found that I was quite free of anti-aircraft fire, for the nearest shells were bursting some three miles away. The Zeppelin was nearly 12,700 feet high and rapidly climbing. I therefore started to dive at her, for although I felt I had a slight advantage in speed, she was climbing like a rocket and leaving me standing. I accordingly gave a tremendous pump at my petrol tank and dived at her firing a burst into her as. I let her have another burst of fire as I passed under her and then banked my machine over and sat on her tail. I fired another burst and could see tracer bullets flying from her in all directions, but I was too close under her for them to concentrate on me.

As I was firing I noticed her begin to go red inside, like an enormous Chinese lantern, then a flame shot out of the front part of her and I realised she was on fire. She then shot up about 200 feet, paused and then came roaring straight down on me before I had time to get out of the way. I nose-dived for all I was worth and expected any minute to be engulfed in flames. I put my machine into a spin, and just managed to corkscrew out of the way in time as she shot past me, roaring like a furnace. I righted my machine and watched as she hit the ground with a shower of sparks. I then proceeded to fire off dozens of green Very Lights, in the exuberance of my feelings.

I glanced at my watch and saw it was about 12.10 am. I then commenced to feel very sick, giddy and exhausted and had considerable difficulty in finding my way to the ground through the fog; in landing I crashed and cut my head on my machine gun.

For this outstanding action against the enemy and not withstanding other difficulties, for example, his aircraft's engine problem, Lieutenant Wulstan Tempest was awarded the Distinguished Service Order. The Zeppelin L. 31 crashed at Oakmere Farm, Potters Bar; again there were no survivors.

Once again the newspapers and media were drawn to Sutton's Farm and their three Zeppelin heroes. Photographs, postcards etc, showing the three airmen's smiling faces adorned shops and houses across the land. The people of Hornchurch, who were especially proud, contributed to a collection to fund special awards to the airmen. On 14th October, at the New Zealand Army Camp at Grey Towers Mansion, Hornchurch, a presentation ceremony was undertaken and three large silver cups were given to Robinson, Sowrey and Tempest by the chairman of the Hornchurch Parish Council W.H. Legg accompanied by Thomas Gardiner JP.

The Germans tried one more airship raid in October 1917, but it was a complete disaster, mainly due to bad weather conditions. A new menace however was looming with the arrival of the German long-range bomber aircraft, the LVG CII, a two seat reconnaissance aircraft, converted to carry 20lb bombs; this had a radius of 200 miles; while the twin-engine Gotha had a crew of three and carried a bomb load of greater capacity.

The first of these aircraft bomber raids took place against London on 28th November 1916, when a LVG CII managed to elude the ground defences, and got as far as the West End of London, dropping six 20lb bombs, but only causing minor damage; there were no fatalities, but six people were injured.

By the time the Home Defence squadrons had been alerted, including Sutton's Farm, who sent up Lieutenant Sowrey at 1.00 pm in his BE12 aeroplane, the German aircraft was already making its return, being sighted near Hastings and the Channel, with no hope of intercepting it.

During the month of December 1916, a pilot known as Captain 'Teddy' Grant arrived at the Headquarters of No. 39 Home Defence Squadron at Woodford, to be shown how the Home Defence Squadrons were organised. The pilot was using a pseudonym, for in reality he was a

Norwegian named Tryggve Gran.

Born in 1888 in Bergan, as a youngster he had travelled the world serving in the navy and later had attended Naval College, finally becoming a naval officer. One of his interests was that of Polar exploration. He became a ski expert and was invited to join the British Antarctic Expedition of 1910 led by Captain Robert Scott. Gran was not chosen to accompany Scott on his ill-fated final trip, but was among the search party that found the frozen bodies of Scott and his two colleagues inside their tent. The cross marking Scott's grave had been constructed by Gran, using his own skis.

When war came in 1914, Gran volunteered to fight for Britain, but as Norway remained neutral, he could only do so by assuming a fake identity, changing his name to Captain Teddy Grant, and his nationality to Canadian.

On 7th December 1916, Gran accompanied Lieutenant Colonel Holt on an inspection of 'C' Flight of 39 (HD) Squadron at Sutton's Farm and during his visit had a memorable meeting with William Leefe Robinson VC. Later that same month, Gran joined 'A' Flight 39 Squadron operating from North Weald Bassett

Lieutenant Frederick Sowrey, who would become the second Zeppelin destroyer based at Sutton's Farm.
Author's collection

The commander of Zeppelin L.32, Oberleutnant Werner Peterson; his airship was one of 11 Zeppelins sent out on the night of 23rd/24th September 1916 to raid Britain. Peterson and his crew would all perish. Albatros publications/Ray Rimell

Lieutenant Sowrey photographed siting in the cockpit of his BE2c biplane along with his two ground crewmen who he said 'should share in some of the glory,' following his victory over Zeppelin L.32.
F. Sowrey collection

Another photograph showing the BE2c of Frederick Sowrey standing outside the wooden hangar sheds for a group photo with the following officers: left to right: Lieutenants Mallinson, Tempest, Captain Bowers, Sowrey and Durstan.

F. Sowrey collection

The crushed remains of one of the L.32's gondolas at the crash-site at Great Burstead, near Billericay.

Author's collection

Lieutenant Wulstan Tempest who would provide the third victory over the Zeppelins from pilots operating from Sutton's Farm in 1916. His victim was Zeppelin L.31, which he brought down over Potters Bar on the night of 1st/2nd October. Author's collection

The commander of Zeppelin L.31 was the vastly experienced and respected 33 year old Kapitanleutnant Heinrich Mathy. He jumped to his death rather than perish in the flames of the falling Zeppelin.

Albatros Publications/ Ray Rimel

The silver presentation cup paid for by donations given to the Hornchurch Parish council that was given to William Leefe Robinson VC for his outstanding bravery and courage on behalf of the village of Hornchurch. In eventuality, two more cups were made and presented for Sowrey and Tempest.

Author's collection

The presentation of the Silver cups took place in the New Zealand Soldiers Convalescent Hospital Camp at Grey Towers Mansion on 14th October 1916. Here we see Robinson and Sowrey with Chairman of the Hornchurch Parish Council, W.H. Legg and Thomas Gardiner JP.

Author's collection

Out for a casual stroll in Sutton's Lane. Three of 39 Squadron's officers, Lieutenants Frederick Sowrey, William Leefe Robinson and Cecil Durstan. It also shows the varying types of uniform worn by the RFC. Robinson is wearing the wrap over tunic which was known as a maternity jacket.   F. Sowrey collection

Date and Hour	Wind Direction and Velocity	Machine Type and No.	Passenger	Time	Height	Course	Remarks
		BROUGHT FORWARD:—		35 HRS. 20 MINS.			
28.VIII.16. 5:35PM	BE.2c.2574 W.			47 MINS.	3,000'	neighbourhood of Sutton's Farm Aerodrome Hornchurch Essex.	Lost aerodrome for a time but found it again.
1.IX.16. 6.30PM	W.	BE.2c.2092	—	25 MINS.	4,400'	Northfleet to Sutton's Farm.	Went to Northfleet as passenger & flew the machine back.
7.IX.16. 6.0PM	N.E.	BE.12.6138	1	20 MINS.	3,000'	Local	
9.IX.16. 6.30PM	N	BE.12.6138	1	20 MINS.	4,500'	To Hainault Farm Aerodrome	
" 7:15 PM	N	BE.12.6138	1	15 MINS.	3,000'	Return to Sutton's Farm	
10.IX.16. 12:30PM	N.N.E.	BE.12.6138	1	25 MINS.	2,000'	Local	Low clouds.
11.IX.16. 7.0PM	W.	BE.12.6138	1	25 MINS.	4,500'	Local	"
13.IX.16. 10.0PM	W.	BE.2c.2092	1	50 MINS.	4,100'	Sutton's Farm to near Southend & back	First night flight. Moonlight.
14.IX.16. 6.0PM	N.	BE.12.6138	1	35 MINS.	8,000'	Pitsea & back	Night flight.
" 10.10 PM	N.	BE.2c.2092	1	20 MINS.	2,000'	Local	Night flight.
16.IX.16 1.0 P.M	N.	BE.2c.4577	1	30 MINS	4,000'	Sutton's Farm to Fort Grain	To take part in practice with airship.
" 2.30PM	N.	BE.2c.4577	1	45 MINS.	2,500'	Isle of Grain	Manoeuvring round airship.
" 3.45 PM	N.	BE.2c.4577	1	20 MINS.	900'	Mouth of River Medway	Dropping Ranken darts on target towed by boat.
" 5.40 P.M.	N.	BE.2c.4577	1	30 MINS.	5,300'	Fort Grain to Sutton's Farm	
19.IX.16. 10.15 A.M	N.W.	BE.2c.4112	1	85 MINS.	4,000'	Mattishall (Norfolk) to Sutton Farm	Collecting machine. Rain. Had storms on the way.
20.IX.16. 6.20PM	N.N.W.	BE.12.6138	1	15 MINS.	3,000'	Local	Testing engine.
21.IX.16. 11:15 AM	N.	BE.12.6138	1	50 MINS.	3,400'	Fort Grain, Southend & back	Engine vibrating.
				44 HRS. 37 MINS.			

A double page extract taken from the log-book of Lieutenant Cecil Durstan who served with No. 39 (Home Defence) Squadron in 1916. It shows that he flew both the aircraft that Sowrey and Tempest flew whilst bringing down Zeppelin's L31 and L. 32. BE2c 4112 and 4577.

Author's collection

Promoted to the rank of Captain, William Leefe Robinson visited the St. Leonards Cottage Home for children and was presented with a souvenir gift. He is pictured here with the chairman of the home and receiving the gift from one of the children dressed in the uniform of the Cottage Home band.

Pathe News Collection

This splendid portrait photograph shows the Norwegian Tryggve Gran, who volunteered to join the Royal Flying Corps and served with No. 39 Squadron and later with 78 Squadron at Sutton's Farm. His own life story read like something out of 'A boy's own adventure novel.'

Borgen Gustav/Norsk Folkemuseum

CHAPTER 4
'Beating the Gotha'

The small raids continued during the first few months of 1917, until towards the end of May, an
then the Gotha's of No. 3 Kahgohl Staffel (Squadron) who were based in enemy–held Belgiur
began their first heavy raids. The first raid was on Folkestone on 25th May which killed 95 people
on 5th June, 22 Gotha's raided as far as Sheerness and Shoeburyness. On 13th June, 14 enem
aircraft got as far as London at 12.10 pm near Liverpool Street Station, Aldgate East and Fenchurc
Street area. The German aircraft dropped a total of 72 100lb bombs, inflicting 162 deaths an
over 400 injured; among the fatalities were 18 children who were killed when their infant schoc
was hit in Poplar.

Pilots from Sutton's Farm were alerted to the raid and two BE12 aircraft took off, flown b
Captain R. Stammers and Captain T. Gran, who sighted the enemy at between 15,000 to 16,00
feet on their return from bombing the capital. They began to chase the bombers from aroun
12,000 feet, firing at them from below as they came into range. As they engaged over Romforc
Stammers aircraft engine began to give him problems and he had to break away from the attac
and head back to Sutton's. Captain Gran continued his attack over the River Crouch, but the faste
Gotha's soon flew out of range, with the BE12s of the RFC totally out-matched by the speed an
armament of the German aircraft.

By the end of June, the Home Defence squadrons were being allocated new aircraft in the forr
of the Sopwith Pup biplane, a faster and more manoeuvrable aeroplane than the BE12, with bette
armament to deal with the Gotha threat. Six of the new aircraft were sent to No. 39 Squadror
while their commanding officer Major R.G. Murrey was replaced by Major J.C. Halahan.

On 5th July, the Norwegian Captain Tryggve Gran was transferred back to 'B' Flight at Sutton
Farm, but there was no spare aircraft for him to fly, so he was given a pass for 48-hours leave
That August, Gran was posted to serve in France briefly with No.70, and then with 101 Squadro
based at Clairmaries.

London was again the target on 7th July, when Gotha's were sighted at 13,000 feet headin
towards the capital, where they dropped 26 bombs. Lieutenant E.S. Moulton-Barrett took of
from the airfield in an SE5, another newly designed faster aircraft and in hot pursuit, he engage
three of the enemy and emptied three drums of ammunition into one of the Germans, but :
seemed to have no effect. Now without any ammunition left, he followed the enemy as far a
Shoeburyness, trying to push their course near to the anti-aircraft guns which were situated there
He returned to the airfield without success.

During this period another squadron was posted to the airfield to help repel the Gotha raids
this fell to No. 46 Squadron, who had been withdrawn from the fighting in France. Led by it
commanding officer Major Philip Babington, it arrived with its Sopwith Pups on 10th July. Thi

rack squadron had also gained the reputation of being airborne from the first news of an alert, n just five minutes. But by August, the squadron was again re-assigned back to the Western Front n France.

It was on the 9th August, that the airfield was visited by the famous flying ace Captain James McCudden and while there received the news of his award of the Victoria Cross, for his outstanding ervice on the Western Front.

Another squadron who had the briefest of stays at Sutton's Farm was No. 66 Squadron. It had eturned to Britain after carrying out ground attack sorties during the Battle of Messines during May. They were then sent to the northern coast of France to try and intercept Gotha raids on their vay to London. Led by the commanding officer Major G.L.P Henderson, they continued the same operations from Sutton's, but after only three days, they were posted back to Belgium to prepare or the second Battle of Ypres and Menin Ridge.

That September of 1917, No. 39 Squadron was posted to operate from North Weald and they vere replaced by No. 78 Squadron. The squadron commander was Major Cuthbert. W. Rowden nd they were equipped with the two-seat Sopwith 1 ½ Strutter, which was soon replaced by the amous Sopwith Camel.

One of the squadron's first engagements with the enemy took place on the night of 25th eptember, when the squadron sent up Captain B. J. Bell on patrol. He was flying a course between he Thames and Joyce Green in Kent, at a height of 9,000 feet, when he sighted and fired upon Gotha bomber. Captain Bell turned his aircraft to pursue the enemy aeroplane, following it astwards for over 15 minutes, firing at intervals as he went, but lost sight of it over the Gravesend rea.

During this same month, the airfield witnessed the first arrival of the women's service, the Women's Legion Auxiliary, the forerunner of the Women's Royal Air Force. They were sent to the irfield to work alongside the men as telephonists, clerical staff and drivers; some of them were illeted at the large country house style building at Breton's Farm, situated between the airfield and Dagenham. Some of the young ladies felt uneasy about their new home, when they were told of umours that the building was haunted.

For the locals, the airfield was always an interesting place to view from the boundary fence, specially for the young boys of that time. Ronald Shelly was one such boy who would visit the irfield many times to see the aircraft taking off. He remembers some of the events he witnessed:

used to get the steam train with my friends to Squirrels Heath Station at Gidea Park, near Romford, and then walk down to Hornchurch Village and then Sutton's Farm. We got down here early one morning, but the hangar sheds were closed, but we were sure that they would do ome flying that day, so we hung around. We then decided to have our packed lunch, when all of sudden the claxon sounded, the hangar doors opened and the machines were wheeled out on o the field. The mechanics warmed them up, and after a while they all took to the air, including Captain Armstrong in his red Sopwith Camel. It transpired that there was a 'Brass hat's meeting,' nd they were given a show; Captain Armstrong did his stunting. I think he got into a bit of rouble because he did one or two really low dives at the officers attending, but to think we would ave missed this, if we had gone home early.

Another afternoon, we saw an RE8 aircraft spinning out of the sky. It crash-landed in an old beetroot field next to the airfield. My friend and I rushed over to where it was. Fortunately for the pilot, he had managed to pull the aircraft up in time to crash horizontally instead of nosing straight in. He was very dazed and we tried to get him out. By that time however, a van had come over from the hangars and they cut open the fuselage and carried him out. I picked up his goggle and helmet as they placed him on a stretcher and I put his stuff on his chest. The pilot said 'What happened? And then he fainted. I later found out his name was Jenkins.

One day at Sutton's, we were sitting near the airfield hedge, when five Bristol fighters came into land, one after the other. By the time the fifth one had got over the boundary hedge, he had sunk a bit too low and he caught his front wheel axle on a small tree stump; his aircraft nosed over smashing the propeller to bits. The pilot got out ok, but his nose was bleeding. The mechanic came running over, and one took the broken prop blade and laid it in the undergrowth saying, I'll come back for that later,' he probably kept it as a souvenir.

I can recall another time, when we walked up one end of the airfield close to a farm. Suddenly a couple of Sopwith Camels came racing low over our heads firing their machine guns at a target in the centre of the aerodrome. It was an exciting experience to see this, one could imagine what it was like with all the noise from the guns and being on the Western Front, but also at the time it was very frightening.

Francis Logan Luxmoore grew up in Weybridge, Surrey, near to the famous motor racing track at Brooklands that also had one of the earliest airfields; it was here that his enthusiasm for flying was triggered. He left Eton in 1916 and joined the Royal Flying Corps. He served with No. 4 Squadron in France and was posted home to England to join No. 78 Squadron in the late summer of 1917. He recalled one event during this period while operating from Sutton's Farm:

Our job was to intercept night raids and we patrolled at varying heights across their paths. But they were very difficult to pick up and there were no search- lights in our area to help us. Only once did I make contact and that was a near collision.

I was near the southern end of my patrol at 11,000 feet, when without seeing him, I crossed in front and slightly below a Gotha returning from London; we only missed each other by a matter of feet. His front gunner saw me because I had the moon behind me and he gave a short burst as I shot by. I whipped my head round just in time to see his starboard wings pass over my tail perilously close. I was purposely flying in a near stalled state, and in my agitation did a half turn of a right-handed spin, which I came out of facing the opposite direction, and then did a right turn which put me on his course.

I knew I had the legs of him and gave charge flat out, and climbing slowly, hoping to pick him out by his exhaust flames. After about two minutes I did, and I proceeded to stalk him. When caught up with him I could see him clearly and got into formation on him at thirty yards just below his slipstream. In that position I had him cold, but when I squeezed the firing lever there was no response, and after further attempts gave it up and peeled away without having been seen.

I was mad and raised hell with the armourers when I landed, without much satisfaction. It was found that the Bowden wire that which operated the interrupter gear had stretched sufficiently o fail the trigger motors of the guns, and I found difficulty in attaching any blame. It was all a isaster for me and I felt it keenly, because in the event of a success it would have represented the rst bomber destroyed over England at night and I would have almost certainly have received an ward.

ollowing his service with 78 Squadron, Luxmoore was posted to No. 37 Squadron and then back o France to serve with No. 54 Squadron. He was shot down over German lines on 18th March 918, surviving the landing to become a prisoner of war and being sent to Holzminden prison amp, where Leefe Robinson was also being held.

At the beginning of March 1918, the Royal Flying Corps had a new aircraft, the Sopwith Snipe, hich was intended to succeed the Sopwith Camel. This new aircraft, one of the prototypes was ent to the airfield and proceeded to give flight demonstrations on 10th March in front of high-nking Royal Flying Corps officers. It was left in the hands of Captain James McCudden VC, who roceeded to throw the machine around the sky with great manoeuvrability.

On 1st April 1918, the Royal Flying Corps became known as the Royal Air Force and during is month, a new night training squadron, No. 189, arrived at the airfield to complement No. 78 quadron.

The Germans mounted their last raid on London on 19th May 1918. One of the Gotha aeroplanes as intercepted by a Sopwith Camel flown by Captain D.V. Armstrong of 78 Squadron, who ngaged the raider just north-west of Orsett, near Tilbury. He dived his machine at the intruder nd fired bursts of machine-gun fire from above and below the enemy aircraft, avoiding the return re from the German rear-gunner. The enemy began to lose height, when it was engaged by nother aircraft, a Bristol two-seater fighter from North Weald, belonging to Sutton's old squadron o. 39. This was crewed by Lieutenant A.J. Arkell and gunner Air Mechanic A.T.C. Stagg, who ow poured more deadly fire into the Gotha. After several minutes, the enemy aircraft burst into ames and headed down, crashing near the Royal Albert Dock, at Roman Road, East Ham.

One new arrival to 78 Squadron during this period was Second Lieutenant Frank Kendall. Born Dalston, London in 1898, he undertook his initial training in 1916 and flew his first solo in ugust 1917. Arriving at Sutton's Farm, he joined 'C' Flight under the command of Lieutenant handler, but was later sent to 'A' Flight led by the famed Captain Armstrong.

During his time there he was involved in testing a Sopwith Camel biplane belonging to No. 189 quadron. Having taken off, and conducting what should have been a routine flight; at 2,000 feet, e main fuel tank exploded soaking Kendall and the aircraft in high octane petrol. He immediately vitched off the ignition and proceeded to put the aircraft down as quickly as possible, breaking e tailskid on landing. His quick thinking had probably saved his life.

He was soon after 'torn off a strip' by his commanding officer for the damage to the aircraft; ut once informed of the young pilot's incident in the air, his commander apologised to him. The use of the accident was that the pressure gauge on the fuel tank had been incorrectly adjusted y a mechanic.

That month also saw the return of Captain Gran, who had returned to active service after being ounded in action whilst carrying out a low level attack on enemy transport near Douai on 30th ovember 1917, and had suffered shrapnel wounds to his left leg. Although badly wounded, Gran with the help of his observer 2nd Lieutenant G.D. Shand had brought their damaged FE2b bac across the Allied lines. For this action Gran was awarded the Military Cross. He was made a fligh commander with 78 Squadron.

During this period, Sutton's Farm was now under the command of No. 49 Wing, whos headquarters were at RAF Upminster, Upminster Hall. The Wing also controlled Hainault Farr and North Weald airfields; its commander was Colonel Malcolm G. Christie.
With no further attacks being made by the Germans, the airfield settled down to a quiet state c readiness, during August and September there was little activity on the airfield.

On Saturday 3rd August, a 'sports meeting' took place at the airfield at 3.00pm, which wa organised by No. 78 and 189 Squadrons, with entertainment supplied by the New Zealand Hospit Band, who were billeted at the Grey Towers Mansion in Hornchurch. The sports programm included tug-o-war, three-legged race, one hundred yards race, a football match and an egg an spoon race and greasy pole. The judges for that day were Major Powell MC and Captain Tryggv Gran MC.

It was also during this period that an inter-squadron competition was organised by the Royal A Force titled 'Squadron in Arms,' which included not only formation flying skills, but also groun maintenance, parade ground drill and wireless telegraphy skills. The competition finals were hel at Sutton's Farm on 22nd September 1918. The winner was No. 141 Squadron from Biggin Hi Kent, whose trophy was awarded to them by Lord Weir of Eastwood and General Ashmore, wh commanded the London Air Defences.

On 11th November 1918 at 11.00 am the Armistice was signed and the First World War ha come to an end, and with it Sutton's Farm's active role in it. What had started out as an experimen with just a small number of men, had ended with an airfield manned by 300 RAF officers an men, and 24 WRAF's; all of them could be proud of what they achieved.

When the task of winding down the Home Defence airfields began, the War Office, lackir foresight, could not see any further use for the continuation of Sutton's Farm, and on 31st Marc 1919, No. 189 (Night Training) Squadron was disbanded. The last squadron to be posted to th airfield after hostilities was No. 51 Squadron who arrived in May 1919, led by Major H.L.H. Owe They were there for less than a month before they too were disbanded. Finally, on 31st Decemb 1919, No. 78 Squadron, the last operational squadron at Sutton's Farm was disbanded.

The land was given back to farmer Tom Crawford, the wooden huts and hangars were tor down, but some of the brick buildings were left standing and used for agricultural purposes.

So ended the short life of one of this country's outstanding airfields of the First World Wa where heroic deeds had taken place and had secured in memory the names of men who had riske their lives in flimsy aircraft at night, with no navigational aids or communication assistance, b who had dealt a huge blow to an enemy trying to break the will of the British civilian populatic through the bombing of their cities. It could be said that this was the first 'Battle of Britain.'

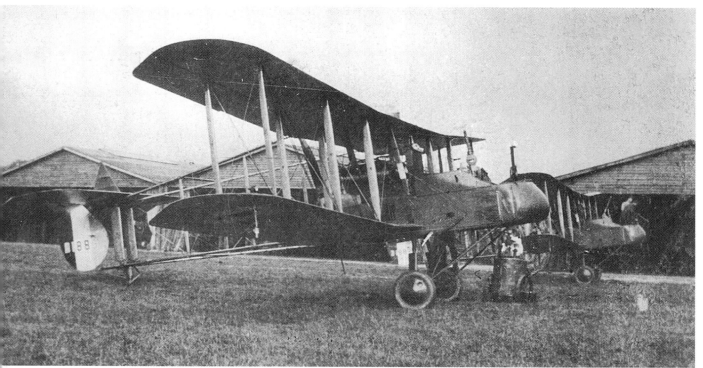

A view of one of the two FE2d aircraft used by No. 78 Squadron. This is B1883. These machines had the engine and propeller mounted behind the pilot's cockpit, while the gunner or observer was seated in the front nose-section. The aircraft were known as 'Pushers'

J.M. Bruce - S. Leslie collection

Ground personnel of 78 Squadron pictured in front of a FE2d pusher biplane at Sutton's Farm in September 1917. These aircraft were replaced by Sopwith 1 ½ Strutters in October that year.

RAF Museum, Hendon

An unidentified officer of No. 46 Squadron pictured next to one of the corrugated buildings on the airfield in 1917. RAF Museum, Hendon

An informal group photograph of Royal Flying Corps officers of No. 46 Squadron relaxing outside one of the huts at Sutton's Farm in August 1917. RAF Museum, Hendon

'Anyone for tennis' An officer of 46 Squadron poses for the camera wearing his tennis trousers and shoes. Behind him stands one of the wooden huts built with a raised brick foundation.

RAF Museum, Hendon

A Sopwith 1 ½ Strutter B762 belonging to No. 78 Squadron pictured here soon after arriving at Sutton's Farm Airfield.

IWM Q 113865

A German Gotha twin-engined bomber pictured in its day-time paint scheme. When their losses over Britain mounted during the daylight raids, they converted to a grey and black camouflage for their missions at night.
IWM Q108846

A brilliant depiction by artist Barry Weekley titled 'Raiders Approach' showing a formation of Gotha G.IV bombers from Kagohl 3 crossing over the coast of England on their way to bomb London.
Barry Weekley collection

Sopwith 1 ½ Strutter A6906 '5' of 78 Squadron is pushed back to the hangars.

RAF Museum, Hendon

Two unidentified officers of 78 Squadron seen pictured with their motor vehicle at a waterlogged and muddy Sutton's Farm during the winter of 1917. Note the substantial brick farm buildings behind the wooden huts.

RAF Museum, Hendon

A group photograph showing the officer pilots of No. 78 Squadron in late 1917, pictured in front of one of the squadron's Sopwith Camels.

Author's collection

This photograph shows the ground personnel of No. 78 Squadron, mechanics, armourers and riggers that kept the squadron operational on the ground as well as in the air.

Author's collection

A Sopwith Pup biplane is pictured with its tail unit raised up on trestles for either repair or alignment or its machine guns.
Author's collection

An unusual visitor to the airfield? This photograph shows a captured German Albatros DV biplane at Sutton's Farm in 1917. The aircraft was flown to various airfields, so that the pilots could inspect what their German opponents were flying.
Author's collection

Captain D.V. Armstrong of 78 Squadron. He engaged a German Gotha biplane on 19th May 1918, near Orsett, Essex. The combat lasted 20 minutes before he broke away. The Gotha was eventually brought down by a Bristol fighter of 39 Squadron and crashed at Roman Road East Ham.   Author's collection

An Avro 504 pictured at the airfield. This aircraft became the main trainer aircraft for the Royal Air Force.   Author's collection

his splendid photograph shows officer pilots of 78 Squadron and the various attire they wore. Those
entified are left to right: Captain Douglas John Bell, Francis Luxmoore, Lieutenant David Greswolde
ewis, the fourth gentleman is unknown.

RAF Museum, Hendon

A 78 Squadron Sopwith Camel stands ready outside one of the hangars on the airfield.

Being prepared for take-off by ground personnel is this line up of No. 78 Squadron Sopwith Camel
In a few minutes they will take to the air.

Captain Douglas Bell of 78 Squadron pictured next to the motor transport at Sutton's Farm in 1917. On the evening of the 25th September 1917, Bell accompanied by 2nd Lt G.G. Williams intercepted a Gotha Bomber south of Brentwood in Essex. After their attack they lost sight of the German, but it later apparently ditched in the North Sea. Bell was credited with 20 victories before he was shot down and killed on 28th May 1918.

RAF Museum, Hendon

ieutenant David Greswolde Lewis of 78 Squadron stands with his Sopwith Camel named 'Rhodesia.' fter serving with 78 Squadron, Lewis was posted to France to 3 Squadron on 29th March 1918. n 20th April, he became the last victim of Manfred von Richthofen, the Red Baron. Lewis was flying opwith Camel B7393 when Richthofen attacked him and set his aircraft alight north-east of Villers- retonneux at 6.43 pm. Fortunately, Lewis survived the crash-landing and spent the remainder of e war as a prisoner.

RAF Museum, Hendon

A quick snap shot for the album, as officers of 78 Squadron entertain a young lady on a visit to the airfield. The aircraft has the words 'Ad Astra painted on the side of the fuselage.   Author's collecti

Sopwith Camels lined up in front of the hangars await the call to become airborne.

Author's collecti

Lieutenant Frank Kendall picture next to his aircraft at Sutton's Farm in early 1918

Frank Kendall's Sopwith Camel biplane B3752 No.6 of 'A' Flight, 78 Squadron 1918

The new Sopwith Snipe fighter Serial No. E8076 pictured at Sutton's Farm under inspection fro[m]
Royal Flying Corps and Royal Navy Air Service officers in March 1918.   L. Bruce collectio[n]

Captain James McCudden VC, th[e]
distinguished flying ace who had score[d]
many victories in the skies over Franc[e]
visited Sutton's Farm on 10th March 191[8]
to demonstrate the flying capabilitie[s]
of the new Sopwith Snipe aircraft. H[e]
was later killed in a flying accident durin[g]
the later stages of the war.

Author's collectio[n]

Officers of No. 78 and No. 189 (Night Training) Squadron pictured at Sutton's Farm in September 1918. Left to right, front row: Wingate, Holking, Kendall, Schmolle, the dog 'Zulu' and Captain Algie.
2nd row: Major Powell, Hyde, Wallis, Walker and Clarke.
3rd Row: Captain Howard, Captain Wolfendale, Attwater, Busher and Finch.
4th row: Perring, Salmond, Murray, Captain Markham, Major Truran. In the doorway: Banner, Captain Law and unknown Brigade Searchlight officer.   W.F. Kendall collection

Sopwith Pup aircraft of No. 189 (Night Training) Squadron, Serial No. 305 at Sutton's Farm in 1918. ote the elaborate paintwork along the fuselage depicting stars.   L. Bruce collection

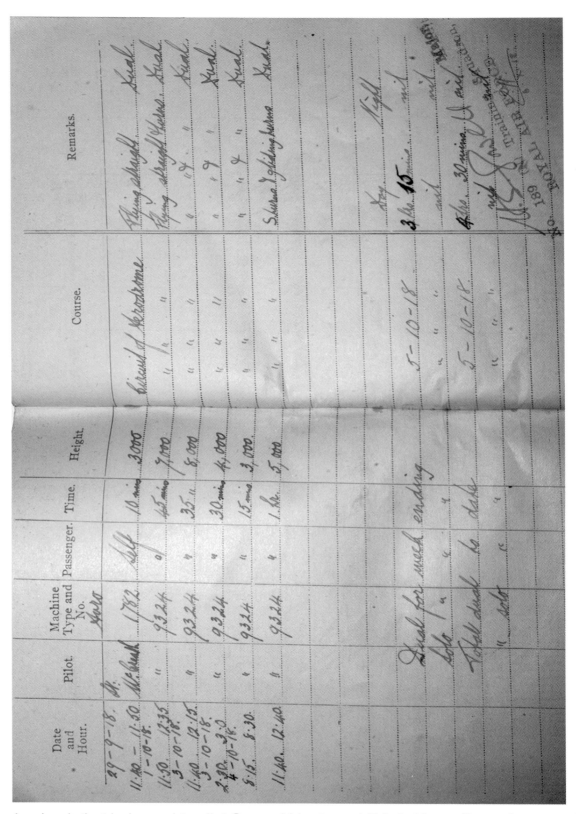

The flying log-book that belonged to pilot Second Lieutenant Edwin Henry Day, who served with N 189 (Night Training) Squadron. It records the flights and the aircraft he flew during this period.

A portrait of Lieutenant Francis Logan Luxmoore who served with 78 Squadron in 1918.

Author's collection

One of the best Royal Flying Corps fighters during the First World War was the SE5a, here is one pictured at the airfield in 1918, serial number B554.

RAF Museum, Hendon

Two ground crewmen are pictured with the remains of a Sopwith Camel which has crashed in an accident at the airfield; they will now have to dismantle the wreck. Author's collection

This relaxed posed shot possibly for a family album shows two young airmen of the Royal Flying Corps who served as ground crew.

Author's collection

Women of the Women's Royal Air Force pictured at Sutton's Farm in 1918, wearing their sky blue uniforms. Miss Grace Hewitson is pictured centre.

Crabtree

Two young ladies of the Women's Royal Air Force sitting at their work desk in one of the wooden huts on the airfield in 1918. Grace Hewitson is pictured on right.

Crabtree

The Breton's Farm Country House, where members of the Women's Royal Air Force were billeted during their time at the airfield. Some of the women felt uneasy staying in the house as someone had stirred a rumour that it was haunted.

Author's Collection

ROYAL AIR FORCE

PROGRAMME OF

SPORTS MEETING

AT

SUTTONS FARM AERODROME

HELD BY THE

78th & 189th SQUADRONS,

ON

Saturday, August 3rd, 1918

AT 3 P.M.

Wilson and Whitworth Ltd., Printers Romford

The programme for a sports event held at the aerodrome on 3rd August 1918.

Author's collection

PROGRAMME OF SPORTS.

78TH & 189TH SQUADRONS.

AUGUST 3rd. 1918.

COMMITTEE.

Judges:

MAJOR POWELL. M.C.
CAPTAIN GRAN. M.C.

Handicappers:

CAPTAIN BARRY.
CAPTAIN BOUMPHREY.
LIEUT. AIGHE. D.S.O.
LIEUT. WILLIAMS.
LIEUT. WALLIS.

Starters:

LIEUT. CLARKE.
LIEUT. CARTER.

Secretary:

LIEUT. HEWER.

Treasurer:

LIEUT. JARVIS.

ITEMS.

1 ONE HUNDRED YARDS, FINAL.
2 GREASY POLE.
3 220 YARDS. FINAL.
4 THREE-LEGGED RACE.
5 FOOTBALL MATCH.
6 ONE MILE, FINAL.
7 OBSTACLE RACE.
8 LADIES' POTATO RACE.
9 TUG-O'-WAR.
10 RELAY RACE.
11 LADIES' EGG AND SPOON RACE.
12 OPEN HALF-MILE RACE.
13 BOOT RACE.
14 BAND RACE.

The New Zealand Hospital Band

By kind permission of the Commanding Officer.

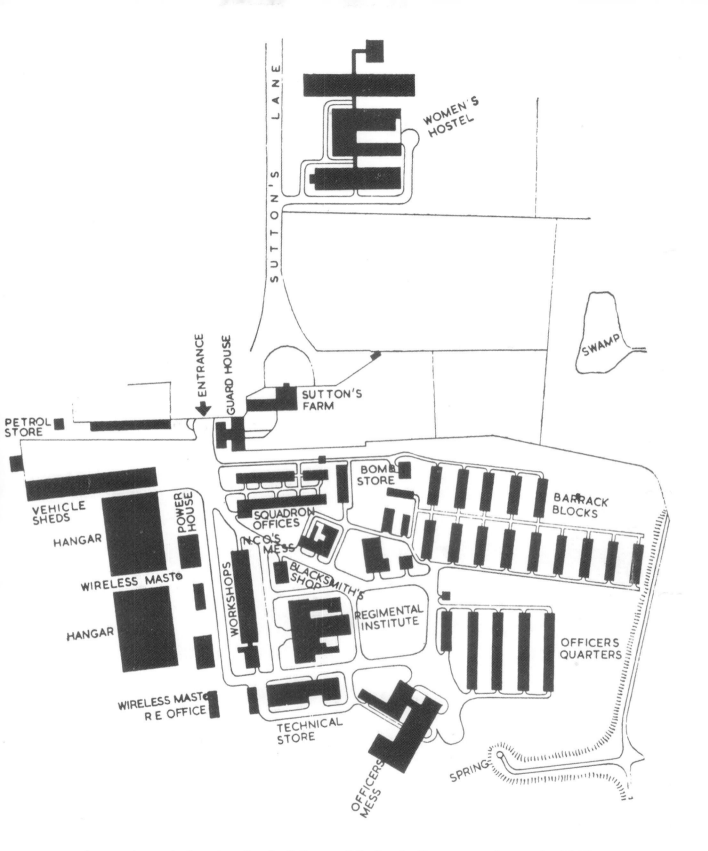

A map layout showing the buildings of Sutton's Farm aerodrome in 1918.

Courtesy of After the Battle Publications

The finals of the Inter-Squadron Competition and the first public demonstration of air-to ground wireless telephony was held at Sutton's Farm on 22nd September 1918 with the winners being No 141 Squadron based at Biggin Hill. Here you can see the demonstration of the wireless telephony being undertaken.   Author's collection

The grave at St. Andrew's Church graveyard Hornchurch of Lieutenant W. A. H. Ellercamp of No. 44 Squadron who was killed over Sutton's Farm when his Sopwith Camel was in collision with another aircraft of 78 Squadron, a Sopwith Snipe flown by Second Lieutenant Hugh Charles Douglas Hurnden on 30th December 1918. Both pilots were killed in the accident.   Author's collection

CHAPTER 5

'Memorabilia'

oday, the artefacts and memorabilia from the First World War are still collected by many
thusiasts, and relics from the battlefields of France and Belgium are still plentiful as farmers
ing to the surface with their ploughs many reminders of the conflict, some items such as shells
d bullets still lethal as they were 100 years ago. Such items from the air war over Britain during
is period are not so common, but do come on to the market and auction sale rooms.
Relics from the Zeppelin airships can sometimes command high prices, but usually are still quite
ailable for those wishing to seek them out.
Thousands of postcards depicting the shooting down of the three Zeppelins by Robinson,
wrey and Tempest were printed at the time, as was photographs of the three heroes and can
quite easily obtained over the internet, but always check the condition. Small pieces of the
eppelins were also gathered at the time and used to raise funds for the Red Cross, the pieces
me within a small envelope printed *In aid of the Red Cross Fund'* and sold for one schilling.
Many other souvenirs from the Zeppelins were picked up by the general public who had rushed
the crash-sites the following morning. These were sometimes made into crosses and brooches
r loved ones and have since been passed down to future generations or left in an old cupboard
d sadly lost in house clearances.
Some larger parts from the Zeppelins airframe sometimes appear on internet sites such as Ebay,
it always check to see if the seller has any provenance to go with the piece.
The following pages show some of the Zeppelin and Sutton's Farm related memorabilia that the
thor has managed to obtain during his collecting over the past 20 years. Happy Hunting!

Recovered from the crash-site of the Schutte-Lanz SL.11, at Cuffley, Hertfordshire shot down ▮ William Leefe Robinson is this air-pressure gauge.

ere are a few pieces of the duralumin metal framework from Zeppelin L.32, which was shot down
Lieutenant Frederick Sowrey on the night of 23rd/24th September 1916. The duralumin was
tremely light metal, but strong and ideal for using as the frame for the giant Zeppelins.

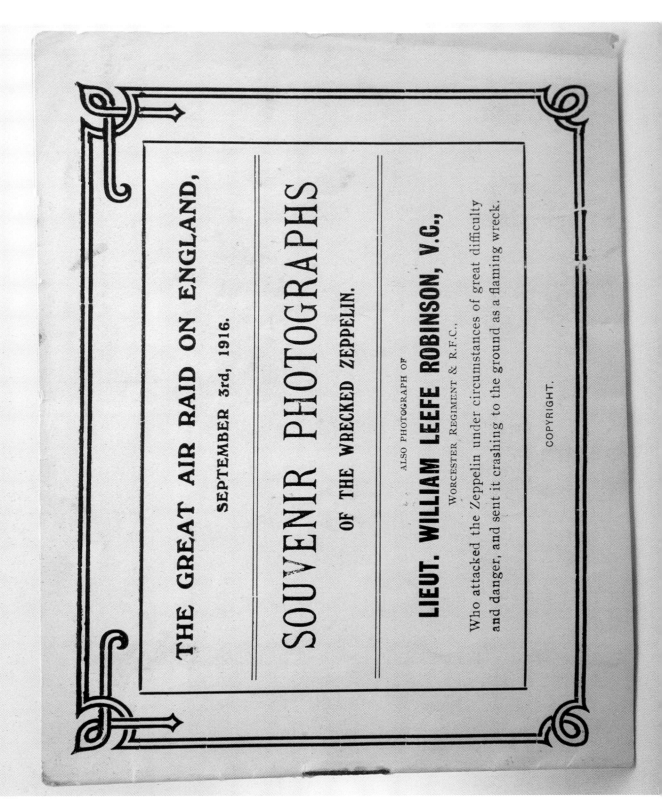

THE GREAT AIR RAID ON ENGLAND,
SEPTEMBER 3rd, 1916.

SOUVENIR PHOTOGRAPHS
OF THE WRECKED ZEPPELIN.

ALSO PHOTOGRAPH OF

LIEUT. WILLIAM LEEFE ROBINSON, V.C.,
WORCESTER REGIMENT & R.F.C.,

Who attacked the Zeppelin under circumstances of great difficulty
and danger, and sent it crashing to the ground as a flaming wreck.

COPYRIGHT.

This small souvenir magazine was printed soon after Robinson had shot down SL.11 and was fi[l]
with many photographs taken of the downed airship's crash-site showing the tangled remains, a[nd]
the story of Robinson's flight and actions that night on 2nd/3rd September 1916.   Author's collec[tion]

78

vo types of metal matchbox covers, which were produced following Leefe Robinson's victory of the rship SL.11. One depicts the shooting down of the airship, the other a portrait of Leefe Robinson VC.

Author's collection

A framed postcard and an envelope with a piece of the wire from the Cuffley airship; which was so
to raise funds for the British Red Cross Society to help the wounded at the front.   Author's collect

is extremely rare piece is the actual compass from Zeppelin L.31 which was shot down over Potters
r by Lieutenant Wulstan Tempest on the night of 1st/2nd October 1916. The compass would have
en situated in the gondola by the main instruments where the steersman was situated. The
mpass was recovered from the crash-site as a souvenir by the officer in charge of the soldiers
arding the crash-site. He gave the compass to his batman to look after. The officer was posted to
ance and the compass remained with his batman, who passed it on to his niece. The author acquired
compass in 2007.

Author's collection

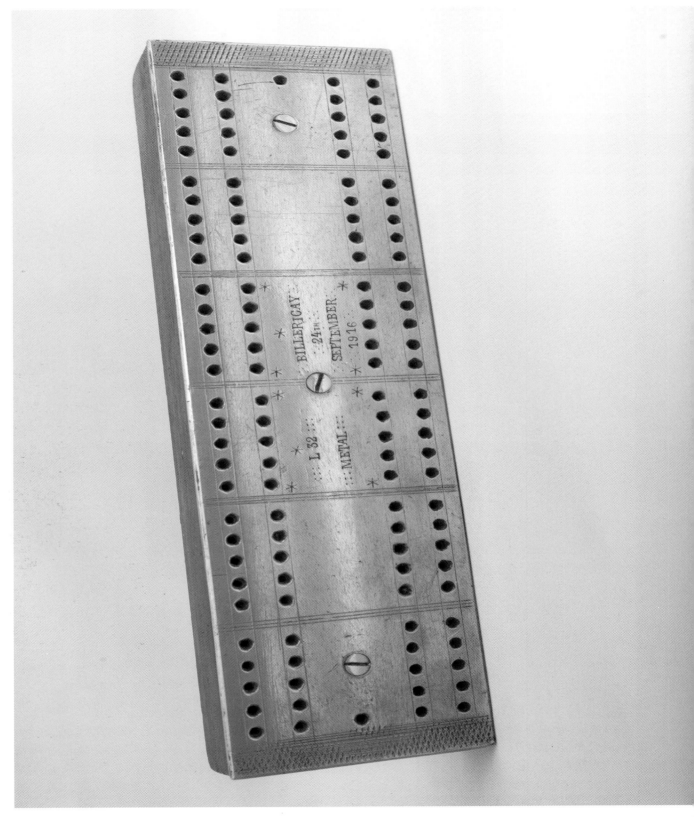

This Cribbage board was made from the remains of the metal recovered from Zeppelin L.3

A postcard of the time depicting the three Zeppelin aces; William Leefe Robinson VC, Frederick Sowrey DSO and Wulstan Tempest DSO.

Author's collection

This photograph shows the remains of a section fibre material that was used to insulate the hydrogen gas cylinders used on the Zeppelin airships.

Author's collection

A small metal dish made from the duralum[in] of Zeppelin L.32. Author's collecti[on]

The remains of some of the data plates fro[m] instruments or engines used on Zeppelin L3[2] brought down at Potters Bar. Due to the he[at] only a few words are still readable.
Author's collecti[on]

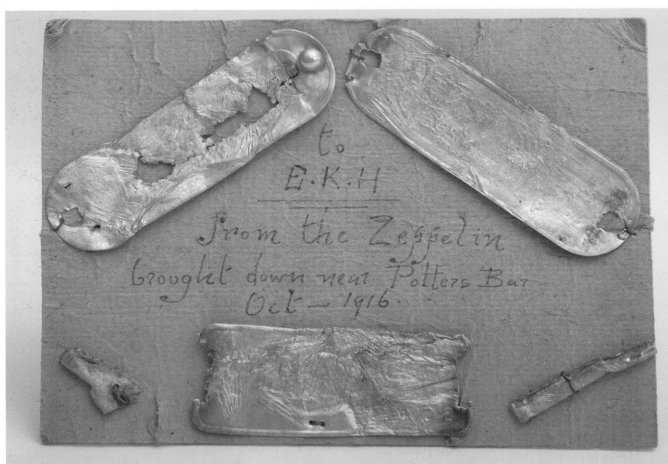

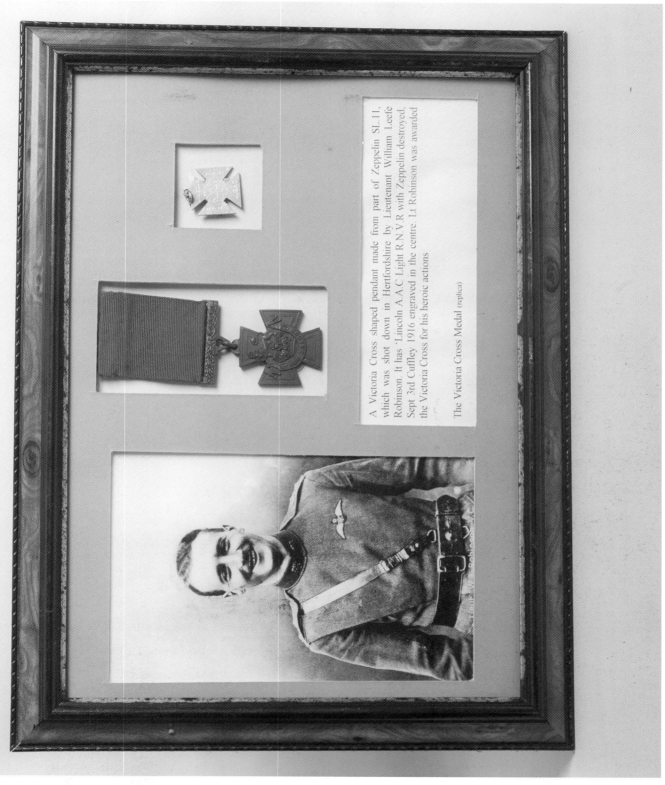

A Victoria Cross shaped pendant made from part of Zeppelin SL.11, which was shot down in Hertfordshire by Lieutenant William Leefe Robinson. It has 'Lincoln A.A.C Light R.N.V.R with Zeppelin destroyed, Sept 3rd Cuffley 1916 engraved in the centre. Lt Robinson was awarded the Victoria Cross for his heroic actions

The Victoria Cross Medal (replica)

This framed piece shows a small memento of a Victoria Cross made from a piece of airship SL.11 (on right) inscribed Lincoln A.A.C Light R.N.V.R, with 'Zeppelin destroyed Sept 3rd, Cuffley 1916. Also framed is a replica Victoria Cross and photo of Leefe Robinson.

Author's collection

This frame carries a certificate of attendance to the Guildhall in London for William Leefe Robinson VC, RFC, to attend the Colonial and Indian Reception Ball.

Author's collection

rare survivor is this souvenir 'Napkin' that was produced by the printer S. Burgess based in the rand, London. The napkin reads 'Souvenir in commemoration of Lieutenant W. L. Robinson's eat Feat in destroying a Zeppelin Sunday Sept 3rd 1916.' 'His greatest reward the heartfelt thanks every woman and child in England.

Author's collection

This is a more current piece of Zeppelin memorabilia, being an original WW1 German soldier's water bottle found on the battlefields of France, but the image of the Zeppelin was painted by artist Ma Kitteridge quite recently. Still a nice piece for Zeppelin collectors.

Author's collecti

The author holds the remains of part of the propeller blade from William Leefe Robinson's BE2c biplane 2693 which crashed in an accident on take-off on the night of 16th September 1916. The piece of prop was taken as a souvenir by James Anderson, who was a civilian carpenter working at the airfield. Anderson was also the landlord of the 'Plough' public house in Cranham; previously he had been a master carpenter for the L.M.S Railway at Stratford. At Sutton's Farm, his job entailed repairing the damaged wooden propellers and parts of framework on the aircraft.

Courtesy of the Barry Anderson collection

No. 78 (Home Defence) Squadron
Roll of Honour

Dedicated to the pilots and airmen killed while flying from Sutton's Farm.

As the longest serving squadron based at Sutton's Farm we remember the following;

2nd Lieutenant Sidney Rex Burton aged 27 – 11th September 1917
Killed when he hit trees on landing whilst flying in Sopwith 1 ½ Strutter B2582
Passenger Air Mechanic 2nd Class S. Rescorla was injured

2nd Lieutenant Aubrey de Teissier – 12th October 1917
Killed whilst flying in Sopwith 1 ½ Strutter A8249.
Crashed following a practice stall on take-off from the airfield

2nd Lieutenant William Hayes Pickup – 12th March 1918
Killed near Sutton's Farm swhilst flying Sopwith Camel C1625.
Whilst practising aerobatics, the aircraft nose-dived into the ground from 1,000 feet.

Captain Sydney Percival Gamon MC aged 23 – 23rd March 1918
Killed near Sutton's Farm aerodrome whilst flying Sopwith Camel C6726
Whilst practising, the aircraft nose-dived into the ground.

Major Cuthbert Roger Rowden MC aged 21 – 20th April 1918
Killed whilst flying in Sopwith Camel C6717
Witness stated 'Bad flying' the aircraft nose-dived into ground

2nd Lieutenant Cyril George Joyce aged 21 – 22nd May 1918
Died from injuries received on 21st May whilst flying Sopwith Camel D6677
Whilst practising aerobatics the engine choked and the aircraft dived into the ground.

Air Mechanic 1st Class John Dunbar aged 29 – 15th July 1918
Accidently killed at Sutton's Farm after being struck by the propeller blade
of Sopwith Camel B9249

2nd Lieutenant Roland Albert James Sadler aged 22 – 23rd September 1918
Killed whilst flying Sopwith Camel C1582
Whilst practising aerobatics, the aircraft dived into the ground

2nd Lieutenant Hugh Charles Douglas Hurndall aged 21 – 30th December 1918
Killed whilst flying in Sopwith Snipe D9459
Whilst conducting a climbing turn, the aircraft collided with Sopwith Camel of
No. 44 Squadron flown by Lieutenant Ellercamp. Both pilots killed.

2nd Lieutenant Hugh Casillis Smith aged 19 – 15th May 1919
Killed whilst flying Sopwith Snipe E8139
Whilst practising aerobatics, the aircraft nose-dived into the ground.

BIBLIOGRAPHY

The following books listed below are of interest to those wishing to know more about the histo
of Sutton's Farm, the Zeppelin raids and RAF Hornchurch in general

Raiders Approach, S/Ldr H.T. Sutton, Gale & Polden 1956
Zeppelins over England, Kenneth Poolman, Evans Brothers Limited 1960
Zeppelin-A Battle for Air Supremacy in WW1, Ray Rimell, Conway Maritime Press 1984
The Airship VC, Ray Rimell, Aston Publications Limited, 1989
Medal for Life, Leslie Bills, Spellmount Limited, 1990
First Thing First, Eric Smith, Ian Henry Publications Limited 1992
Zeppelin Volume 2, Ray Rimell, Albatros Productions Ltd 2008
The First Blitz, Neil Hanson, Transworld Publishers, 2008
Hornchurch Scramble, Richard C. Smith, Grub Street 2000
Hornchurch Offensive, Richard C. Smith, Grub Street 2001
Hornchurch Eagles, Richard C. Smith, Grub Street 2002
Second to None, A pictorial history of Hornchurch aerodrome 1915-1962, Richard C. Smith,
Grub Street, 2004
Hornchurch Streets of Heroes, Richard C. Smith, Mitor Publications, 2013

For further information on books or DVDs by Richard C. Smith visit the website

www.mitorpublications.co.uk

Other titles available from Mitor Publications

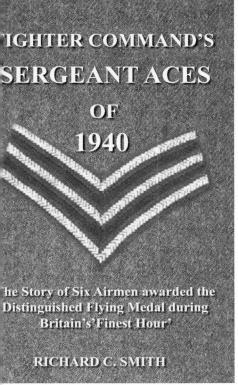

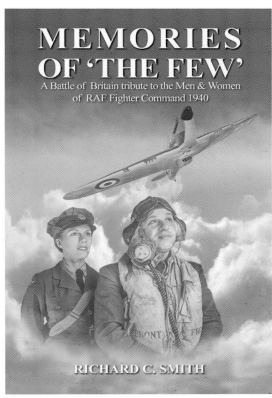

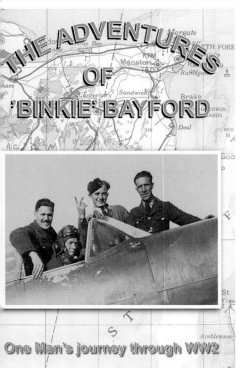

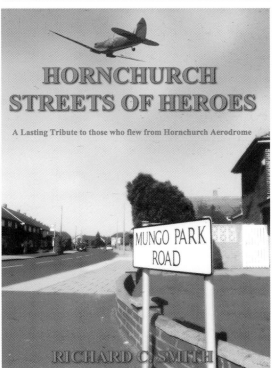